Chess Mate - Unpacking Chess with rhymes

Riz Ahmed

BookLeaf Publishing

India | USA | UK

Presentation by *BookLeaf Publishing*

Web: www.bookleafpub.com

E-mail: info@bookleafpub.com

ISBN: 9789358313161

First edition 2023

To my Goji Berry

Love Maa

What is Chess?

What is chess, you may wonder and ask?
It's a game of strategy, a captivating task.
With kings and queens, knights so grand,
Let's explore this game, so you understand.

Chess is a puzzle, a battle of the mind,
A chance to be wise, thoughtful, and kind.
It's good for learning, for young and old,
Developing skills, both brave and bold.

It teaches patience, a virtue so rare,
and helps with decision-making, with thought
and care.
Chess is a friend that's always there,
To challenge your wits, to play and to share.

It's a game of rules, where fairness prevails,
Where every move counts, and the story unveils.
In the world of chess, you'll learn and explore,
With friends or alone, there's always more.

So, what is chess? It's a world of delight,
A board of adventure, from dawn until night.
Good for your mind, and friendships it will
bring,
Chess is a game that can make your heart sing!

Origins of Chess

In lands of old, where legends unfurled,
Chess, the timeless game, has spanned the
world.
A history rich, with tales to tell,
Of strategy and battles, where empires rose and
fell.

It began in India, over a thousand years ago,
as "chaturanga," where four armies would go.
Elephants, chariots, cavalry, and infantry,
The pieces in play, with grand strategy.

Through Persia, it spread, with the name
"shatranj,"
to the Islamic world, where minds would
embark on this plan.
The game evolved, with new rules to embrace,
And across borders, it continued to grace.

To Europe, it journeyed, as chess came to life,
The medieval courts with nobility rife.
With queens, knights, bishops, the game took its
form,
As it gained its structure, with every move and
norm.

Through centuries and battles, and strategies
refined,
Chess became a contest of heart, soul, and mind.
Innovations and tactics, as it grew and improved,
A game of wit and wisdom, where many hearts
moved.

Today, in every corner, on a board of sixty-four,
Chess continues its legacy, rich at its core.
With lessons of patience, strategy, and grace,
The history of chess is a captivating embrace.

So as you play on, with pieces in hand,
Know that chess has a story, an ancient grand.
A game for the ages, with a heritage so vast,
In the world of chess, the adventures will last.

Chess through the times

In ages past, where time did unfurl,
A game emerged, a cerebral swirl.
Chess, the ancient tale it weaves,
A saga of thinkers, of kings, and eves.

In India's embrace, it found its start,
Chaturanga, a game, a strategic art.
Elephants, chariots, knights, and more,
On a battlefield board, they'd explore.

To Persia's courts, it then did roam,
Shatranj, with strategy to comb.
Across the Silk Road, its journey took flight,
Chess pieces dancing in the Arabian night.

To Europe's castles, it gracefully strode,
With queens and bishops, a royal code.
The medieval board, a chessman's domain,
A game of wits, a nobleman's gain.

Through centuries, it evolved and refined,
Chess, a masterpiece, of every kind.
From pauper to king, it captured the heart,
A game where tactics and cunning impart.

In this chessboard realm, where stories take flight,
Pieces move, in a dance of might.
From ancient whispers to the present cheer,
Chess, a timeless game, we hold dear.

Benefits of Chess

In the realm of chess, where wisdom aligns,
A world of benefits, where intellect shines.
With every move, a strategy to weave,
Let's explore the wonders that chess can achieve.

In the dance of the pieces, the mind takes flight,
As young players ponder, their skills ignite.
Patience, a virtue, chess teaches so well,
In this grand game where moves tell and tell.

Decision-making, a skill to enhance,
Each move, a choice, a thoughtful advance.
Critical thinking, a knight's noble ride,
In the world of chess, where minds open wide.

Concentration, like a rook's steady tower,
Focused and sharp, hour after hour.
Memory skills, a bishop's keen sight,
Recalling the board, every move, every fight.

In the chessboard's embrace, where friendships
can bloom,
Respect and sportsmanship, not just in the room.
A game of respect, where manners play,
In victory and defeat, in every chess day.

So, young players, take up the chess quest,
In this royal game, where you'll be your best.
For in the kingdom of chess, benefits are seen,
A world of wonder, where minds reign supreme.

Sportsmanship

In the chessboard's realm, where kings and queens convene,
A noble code of conduct, a sportsmanship sheen.
As pieces dance and strategies align,
Let's explore the spirit, both yours and mine.

In victories sweet, with checkmate's embrace,
Or defeats bitter, where pieces find space,
A handshake or nod, with a genuine smile,
Chess sportsmanship thrives, mile after mile.

Win or lose, it's the game we adore,
Respect for the opponent, forevermore.
In the chess kingdom, where fairness prevails,
Each move tells a story, as the chess tale sails.

No taunts, no boasts, no ill-willed jest,
But a gracious demeanor, in victory's crest.
For in this chessboard ballet, where minds compete,
Sportsmanship reigns supreme, in every seat.

So, young chess players, let honour be your guide,
In the game of chess, where friendships abide.

A knightly code, a queenly grace,
In the game of chess, sportsmanship takes its
place.

The Pawn

In a chess game grand, with pieces galore,
Pawns stand in the front row, ready for the war,
Little foot soldiers, brave and true,
Let me tell you what these pawns can do.

They march ahead, one step at a time,
In front of the army, they form a line,
Simple and small, but with hearts so bold,
Guarding the kingdom, come young and old.

Yet, when pawns reach the other side,
A special transformation, they can't hide,
Becoming queens, powerful and strong,
Their journey in the game, oh so long.

So remember, young players, don't
underestimate,
The humble pawn, its changing fate,
In chess, they prove that even the small,
Can rise to greatness, stand tall.

The Pawn

In the chess world so vast, where battles are
bold,
There's a piece known as the pawn, brave and
quite old.
Though small in stature, it has a secret to share,
How it can capture others, with moves so fair.

A pawn moves forward, just one square at a
time,
But on its first move, it can leap, it can climb!
Two squares ahead, it can go in a dance,
Then, diagonally, it captures with a chance.

So, young chess players, don't underestimate,
The humble pawn's skill, it's truly great.
With its simple moves, it plays its part,
In the grand chess game, it's a clever work of art.

A pawn can be a hero, in its special way,
Capturing pieces, and winning the day.
In the world of chess, where tactics compete,
Even pawns can taste victory, in their feats so
sweet!

The Rook

In the land of chess, where battles are staged,
The rook stands strong, never to be caged.
With turrets on top, like a castle so grand,
Let's explore the rook's role in this royal land!

It moves like a rocket in a straight line,
Horizontally or vertically, either is fine.
The rook's role in chess, it's simple and clear,
To protect and defend, it's always near.

In castles and towers, it's the ruler's delight,
Guarding the kingdom both day and night.
With its power to roam, and its strength so vast,
In the game of chess, it's unsurpassed.

It joins forces with the King in a move called
"castling,"
A strategic dance, their safety encapsulating.

So remember, young players, in this chessboard
scene,
The rook's vital role, like a chessboard queen.
With straight-line moves, and a fortress to tend,
In the game of chess, it's a loyal friend!

The Rook

In the chessboard's grand and checkered domain,
The rook is a sentinel, its role is quite plain.
With turrets atop, like a castle so stout,
It guards and it moves without a doubt.

Along rows and columns, it strides with might,
A straight-line roamer, a powerful sight.
No diagonal jaunts for this steadfast tower,
Its moves are resolute, its strength is its power.

It guards the king, and it helps in the fight,
In castles and kingdoms, both day and night.
With its ally, the king, in a special embrace,
They castlingly journey to a safer space.

In the realm of chess, it's a guardian bold,
A rook's steadfast presence, a story unfolds.
In its straight-line path, it stands firm and true,
In the game of chess, there's no piece quite like
you!

The Bishop

In the chess kingdom, where pieces abide,
The bishop's a character with a unique stride.
With a hat like a mitre, he's a sight to behold,
Let's discover the bishop, brave and bold!

He moves on the squares, diagonally his way,
In his own colour zone, he loves to sway.
One bishop wears white, the other wears black,
Their mission is clear, no courage they lack.

They protect the kingdom with a holy grace,
In this chess world, they find their place.
Their watchful eyes, sharp and keen,
Guide the pieces through battles, in your
chessboard scene.

In this chessboard realm, where tactics are
profound,
The bishop's role in strategy does astound.
Diagonally they roam, with wisdom to bear,
In the world of chess, they're a royal pair!

The Knight

The knight, a character, both daring and bold.
With a horse's head and a gallant prance,
Let's delve into the knight's unique chess dance.

In an L-shaped stride, it takes the lead,
Two squares forward, then one to succeed.
Over pieces it jumps, in a whimsical flight,
A knight's journey, a strategic delight.

Through battles and skirmishes, it ventures with
glee,
A chessboard knight, wild and free.
Its moves unpredictable, like a noble quest,
In the game of chess, it truly is the best.

So young players, take heed of the knight,
With its L-shaped move, both cunning and
bright.
In the chessboard's realm, where stories
convene,
The knight's move, a dance, majestic and keen.

The Queen

In the realm of chess, with strategy grand,
The queen reigns supreme, the most powerful
hand.
She's royalty on squares of black and of white,
With moves so versatile, she's a dazzling sight.

She glides through the board, with grace and
with flair,
In any direction, she moves with great care.
Horizontally, vertically, diagonally, she goes,
Her reach is unmatched, her power grows.

With her regal presence, she guards the domain,
Supports her allies, and creates a campaign.
Her role in the game is simple but grand,
To dominate the board and defend the land.

The queen's the true star of this chess ballet,
She's the one you protect, in every game you
play.
With her strength and her smarts, she's a
formidable force,
In the game of chess, she sets the course.

So when you're in battle, in this royal contest,
The queen's role in chess, remember it best.
She's the monarch's right hand, with a power so
keen,
In the grand game of chess, she's a majestic
queen!

The Queen

In the kingdom of chess, where battles unfold,
The queen reigns supreme, a story untold.
With a crown on her head and a regal gaze,
Let's delve into the importance of her chessboard
phase.

She moves with grace, in any direction she'll fly,
A powerful force, reaching for the sky.
Horizontally, vertically, diagonally so keen,
The queen commands the board, a majestic
queen.

Her role is vital, in the royal scheme,
A powerhouse, like a chessboard dream.
With tactics and strategy, she shapes the play,
Guiding her pieces in a calculated array.

She guards the kingdom with a watchful eye,
A protector, as pawns and pieces vie.
In battles of chess, she takes the lead,
A majestic force, on her noble steed.

So, young players, in this chessboard array,
Learn from the queen in the grand chess ballet.
In the game of chess, her importance is seen,
The queen, a royal piece, in every chess queen.

The King

In the kingdom of chess, with pieces in play,
The king holds the crown in a regal display.
He's not the mightiest, but his role is divine,
For without him, the game cannot shine.

He moves just one step, in any direction he's
free,
Yet his safety's paramount, as you will soon see.
He's the centrepiece, the heart of the game,
And protecting the king is the ultimate aim.

Check and checkmate, the threats are so real,
The king must evade every strategic ordeal.
With the help of his rook, in castling they blend,
To find refuge and safety, a fortress to defend.

Though he may be frail, in the grand chess array,
The king's the true monarch, come what may.
In the game's noble dance, his role is serene,
For without the king, there's no chessboard
scene.

So remember, dear players, in each noble match,
The king's role in chess, with a royal dispatch.
He's the reason we play, the heart of the thing,
In the world of chess, long live the king!

Check

As the games goes on, where strategies spin,
Comes a move called "check," let the games
begin!
It's a moment of warning, a royal decree,
A signal to the king, "Watch out, it's me!"

A piece makes a move, an attacking delight,
Putting the king in a precarious plight.
The monarch's in danger, but worry not,
There are ways to escape, a strategic thought.

The queen, the rook, or a knight's surprise,
They put the king in a tactical guise.
With clever moves, the danger may fade,
And the king, unharmed, can still evade.

So, young chess adventurers, when check is
near,
Think and plan, hold onto your cheer.
In this grand chess game, where tactics entwine,
The role of check is a challenge, both yours and
mine!

Checkmate

In the land of chess, where battles unfold,
Comes a moment of triumph, a story retold.
It's called checkmate, the ultimate prize,
A thrilling finale, where victory lies.

The king's in a trap, he can't escape fate,
It's a royal defeat, it's checkmate!
A clever maneuver, a strategic ploy,
Leaves the king defenseless, with no joy.

The pieces align, like stars in the night,
The queen, the knight, in checkmate's sight.
The king can't move, he's in dire straits,
A triumphant moment, that truly elates.

With checkmate declared, the game is complete,
The victor stands tall, in their chessboard seat.
So young chess enthusiasts, learn and create,
The art of chess and the thrill of checkmate!

Stalemate

In the world of chess, where strategies abound,
There's a special ending, not victory nor a frown.
It's called a stalemate, a different kind of fate,
Let's explore this twist, it's truly great!

When the king is not in check, yet he can't
move,
No legal moves left, no tactics to prove.
It's a tie, a draw, where both players agree,
Neither can win, but they're both set free.

The pieces stand still, in a frozen dance,
No attacks to launch, no moves left to enhance.
It's a peaceful conclusion, in a chessboard quest,
A stalemate declared, both players at rest.

So remember, young chess champs, in this royal
game,
A stalemate can happen, it's not the same.
As a win or a loss, it's a different state,
A unique outcome, it's the art of stalemate!

Castling

In the game of chess, where tactics conspire,
There's a move called castling, which players
admire.
Two pieces in harmony, a king and a rook,
They come together in a clever hook.

The king seeks safety, a fortress to find,
To protect against threats of every design.
With a trusty rook, by his sturdy side,
They perform castling, in this game of pride.

The king makes a move, just two squares to the
side,
While the rook, with a leap, takes a royal ride.
They swap their positions, in a strategic dance,
Creating a fortress, a chessboard romance.

It's a move of defense, a tactic so wise,
A way to ensure the king's safety belies.
In the game of chess, it's a brilliant maneuver,
Protecting the monarch, with moves so clever.

So remember, young players, in each chess
game's thing,
The power of castling, how it makes kings sing.

A strategy, a dance, in this grand chess show,
With castling's embrace, the king's safety aglow!

En Passant

In the chessboard world, where strategies sway,
There's a move called en passant, a trick at play.
Let's uncover this tactic, both simple and neat,
In the game of chess, it's a move hard to beat!

When a pawn moves forward two squares at a
time,
And lands beside an enemy in its prime,
The capturing pawn takes its chance, it's the key,
To capture en passant, and that's a strategy!

With a swift sideways move, the pawn's caught
in flight,
As if it had moved just one square in sight.
It's a surprise manoeuvre, a pawn's quick
advance,
En passant is a move that can make you dance.

So young chess learners, remember this skill,
En passant can come in handy, it surely will.
In the chessboard's dance, where tactics are
meant,
Master en passant, and you'll be competent!

www.ingramcontent.com/pod-product-compliance
Lightning Source LLC
La Vergne TN
LVHW051249200726